The Sanskrit words Bhagavad Gita are translated in English as Song of God.

If you would like to receive a complimentary copy of another book by Kathy go to VIVAPAX.com

KRISHNER IN NEW YORK

A New Bhagavad Gita

Kathy Braun

VIVA PAX

TRUDY'S DESPAIR

1. Trudy Newman awoke
Feeling thoroughly rotten
All joy she'd once had
Completely forgotten

2. The thoughts in her head
All served to depress her
The 8 AM News
Was more of a stressor

3. Harry Krishner the name
Of the driver today
Trudy hopes that he'll
Have nothing to say

4. Just turn on the meter
And drive, driver, drive
(Oh God, I wish that
I weren't alive!)

5. Harry Krishner responds,
Pardon me, Miss,
Don't be offended
But I must address this

6. Oh God, Trudy thought,
He's heard what I said
Well alright and yes,
I wish I were dead

7. I'm sick of this life
   Sick unto death
   I want no more life
   I want no more breath

8. So many people I meet
Are so mean
So much of life
Just seems obscene

9. They know how to fight
They know how to boast
They know how to grab
What will get them the most

10. They trash the world
For all its worth
Pollute the water,
Sky and earth

11. Just look around
What do you see?
Lives that revolve
Around getting that fee

12. That's what they care about,
Credit or cash
It's all about money
All the same trash

13. Dollars, long green,
The almighty buck
For it, their grandmother's eyes
They would pluck

14. And you don't need a genius
To make the deduction
That leaders can just lead
The way to corruption

15. People are virtually
Steaming with greed
If we go on this way,
Where will it lead?

16. They darken the sky,
They poison the water
People don't act
The way that they oughta

17. They're killing the places
The animals live
They know how to take
But not how to give

18. It once was said
And it still means a lot
"Take Paradise,
Put up a parking lot!"

19. Krishner replied:
Now don't think me odd
But my question to you is
What about God?

20. Oh yeah yeah, right, sure,
It's all in God's plan
Well, tell me who's worse then,
This God or His man?

21. This God that you name
Means nothing to me
How can I believe in
What I can't see?

22. But of course you see God,
Take me for example,
This chat that we're having
Is just one small sample

23. Of all I can do,
But I'm here and I'm real,
What more do you want?
Don't you find this ideal?

HARRY KRISHNER, NY CHARIOTEER

24. I'll take you
Where you want to go
And teach you
What you want to know

25. Harry Krishner,
NY charioteer
When things get bad,
I reappear.

26. Caught by surprise,
But now less despondent
She inhaled and exhaled
And then she responded

27. Harry, you're showing
A kind of pathology -
God is a construct,
Essential mythology

28. Oh sure we're all here,
But not in defiance
Of all that we know
And what's proven by Science

29. A cabdriver God proxy
Is so...so archaic -
The truth is
We're deoxyribonucleic

30. Deoxy...wow!
What a word! I'm impressed!
So how come Miss Smarty,
You're still so depressed?

31. Science is great
But not the right knowledge
For that which you seek.
Enroll in my college.

32. For you, Trudy dear one,
Sweet senorita,
Attend to my teaching
I've turned off the meter.

33. For I am everywhere:
The food you eat,
The autumn trees,
The summer heat

34. The boundless reach
Of outer space
As close to thee
As thy own face

35. I am the beginning, the end,
And all in between
I see all the evil,
I make all things clean

36. I am the leaves, the flower,
The stem and the root
The beauty, the color,
The fragrance, the fruit

37. From me to the plant,
Then to you, I'm nutrition
I am the total and final
Sum of addition

38. I'm the tiniest part
Of all things divisible
I'm all that you see
And all that's invisible

39. I'm music itself,
Tis I call the tune
I am the Word,
I rhyme moon with June

40. I'm the muse of the artist,
The canvas, the paint
Trudy, the fact is
There's nothing I ain't

41. Getting to know Me,
Feel sure that you're bound to
Transform yourself
And turn life around too

42. Fight the good fight Tru,
I know you can do it
I'm God after all
And this I intuit

43. Listen here Harry
Don't get me wrong
I'm loving your pure Krishner's
New York God-song

44. If God is around
And you really can show it
There's nothing on earth I'd prefer
Than to know it

45. This taxi I know you can move it,
You see,
But God - well, how can you
Prove that to me?

46. Tru, you make a mistake
To place your reliance
On something as small
And as fragile as science

47. Science can know
What's open to measure
But cannot unlock
True measureless treasure

48. The study of science
In order to move
Is rightly concerned
With wanting to prove.

49. The proof you require
Is a function of math
Just right for its use
But no spiritual path

50. It's like trying to prove
That true love is real
It surely exists,
But it's something you feel

51. Sorry, but science
Can't help here because
Science will never be able
To figure First Cause

52. The knowledge of God
Is a whole other thing,
It lies deep within you
A pure hidden spring

53. I cannot be known
Except for the part
Of Divine Life Itself
That resides in your heart

54. For "I Am That I Am"
Is within every human
Including yourself,
My dear Trudy Newman

PERFECT PEACE

55. To find your own
Individual answer
You must become
A spiritual dancer

56. And move to the beautiful
Sound of one's spirit
With first the will to listen
And then the will to hear it

57. A method to use
(Though it goes out of fashion)
Is: take hold of yourself,
Encourage dispassion

58. Seek to develop,
Have as a goal:
The kindly heart,
The loving soul

59. Who looks with compassion
And not with disgust
At the weakness in all
Since all of us must

60. Play out our parts
On our too human stage.
While beyond all the sorrow,
The anger, the rage

61. Lies deep, perfect peace.
It's there if you will
Quiet your mind
And become very still.

62. Open yourself
To deep meditation -
God's way of engaging
In sweet conversation

63. Our nature is joy
Our nature is peace
When you finally can get
The mind's clamor to cease

64. If thou wouldst
Attain divinity,
Cultivate
Thy equanimity

65. If you kill yourself
And all that you're worth,
Are you different from those
Who are killing the earth?

66. If your exit from life
Is self-done and abrupt,
Are you different from those folks
You label corrupt?

67. To give in to the dark
To give in to despair
To extinguish the Newmanesque
Light that is there...

68. Is...Trudy, you with me?
I repeat...(pause)...ahem!
Is to transform yourself
To the famed loathsome them.

69. Your self and some others
Need some forgiving
Who's there to do it
If Newman's not living?

70. Finding the courage
To act as you should,
Working each day
For the sake of the good

71. Willing to drop
The cynical mask
And simply be good,
Why that's a brave task!

72. Life is a miracle,
Easy to see it
The hard part is finding
The way you can be it

73. If you give up the anger
And give up despair
And look for the peace
That always was there

74. Beyond all the fear,
The sorrow, the rage,
Is a place to be free
Of this bodily cage

MYSTERY

75. Trudy, dear one
Of course you have doubt
No creature that lives
Can figure me out

76. Creator of life,
Author of history
Sometimes they call me
Ms./Mr. Mystery

77. Why hasten your death?
You'll just come around again
Stay with it Tru,
You'll be perfectly sound again

78. Wait, Harry, wait,
Have I heard you right?
Do I get what you're saying?
Do I see in the light?

79. When you say, Harry Krishner,
Are you giving me then
The startling info
That I'll live again?

80. Look here Tru,
With inner eye
You can truly
Never die

81. That by which
All this is pervaded
Cannot be destroyed,
Cannot be evaded

82. These bodies we're housed in
Are the external
Of That which pervades
And is truly eternal

83. It can't be destroyed,
It never will perish
It's changeless, immeasurable -
That which we cherish

84. It's called by ten thousand
Different names
But it's That which pervades,
Which is always the same

85. Dear one, your body's
   But a habitat
   For what's within,
   For Thou art That

86. All that science
Understands
Is smaller than
A grain of sand

87. But Trudy,
Don't get too dispirited
The nature of science
Is that it's limited

88. It needs to be slow,
To be sure and conservative
Methods appropriate
As a preservative

89. But I give science
A break now and then
As slowly my workings
Dawn upon men

90. And rebirth will one day
Be understood
As man further realizes
All of God's good

91. You are eternal,
It simply is true
Let the heart know
What the mind cannot do

THE VISION

92. I can't help it, Harry,
Though I know you are wise
I was born to see
With my own New York eyes

93. Trudy, New Yorker,
I've just made a decision
Look deep in my eyes,
I give you this vision

94. Behold Trudy, then,
See My total divinity
My forms in their millions
And on into infinity

95. A million mouths,
   A million eyes
Decked with garlands,
   Weapons high

96. Terrible
With many jaws.
Filled with terror
Trudy saw

97. The brilliance
Of a million suns -
The universe
Perceived as One

98. The gnashing of teeth,
The flashing of claw,
The armies that march,
All this Trudy saw

99. Armies, nations,
No one spared,
All by God
As Time ensnared

100. Tens of millions
Staring skulls,
Empty carcass,
Empty hulls

101. Ten million births
With babies screaming
Species dying,
Planets teeming

102. Please Harry stop,
I really can't take it
I know now
You're not just trying to fake it

103. This vision of God
I now apprehend
Has set me to tremble,
My hair stands on end

104. Oh Harry please
Be my driver again
And not fiery Time,
Devourer of men

105. Oh Krishner I cannot
Cope with your might
I'm just a small human
With small human sight

106. Oh God You are real
You are real, You are real!
No more, Harry please.
I need time to heal.

107. Trudy dear one,
I gave you this vision
So you'd know it was Me
And for sure, with precision

108. Birthless, deathless,
And changeless am I
But real and not some
Imagined sci-fi

109. I am in all
And all is in Me -
We all always were
And will always be

110. Every soul will
Come to see
That every soul
Is part of Me

111. No matter what
Their line of thought
They're all a part
Of what I've wrought

112. As rivers
All return to sea
So all souls
Return to Me

113. Never was I not,
Nor Thou, nor Them
From the lowest of the low
To the crème de la crème

114. This body can't choose
To escape certain death
Or extend its stay earthbound
By even one breath

115. Nobody gets out of here
Alive
Not one body
Will survive

116. The body is fleeting
And so is the mind
But the soul is eternal
And Trudy, you'll find

117. If you put your devotion
Centered on Me
You'll locate that part of Me
Which is Thee

118. Oh yes I'm real,
Be totally sure
Therefore my dear one,
My loved one, endure

CHOICE

119. Quiet your mind,
Stay firm in devotion
To Me, and don't be a slave
To emotion

120. On the path to reach Me
You must be meticulous
And not be entrapped
By sensory stimulus

121. God is a word
For what can't be described
But a piece of the puzzle
Can be prescribed

122. One certainty gives us
Cause to rejoice
We're all of us blessed
With freedom of choice

123. Among the fine gifts
God gives us to use
Is our tiny but crucial
Margin to choose

124. We can seek to contribute
Or seek to abuse
God asks of us all -
Which do you choose?

125. We can seek the divine
Or live out the blues
It comes right back to -
Which will you choose?

126. Trudy, hear
A new beatitude
Blessed be
The righteous attitude

127. Aim high and see,
You'll be sure to achieve it
Reality's shaped partly
By how you perceive it

128. Fight sorrow, fight anger,
Fight negativity
Be born of compassion,
And find new nativity

129. The self is your enemy,
The self is your friend
Whichever prevails,
On your choices depend

130. But Krishner,
Sometimes I feel
So very alone
Don't worry my girl,
God answers the phone

131. A lighthearted way
Of saying it's true
That nothing there is
Can be closer to you

132. Than that Holy of Holies
Which always resides
Just where you can find It,
Safely inside

133. But Harry, there's still
The matter of evil
Is it part of our nature,
Ancient, primeval?

134. Immune to our ongoing
Efforts to change it
No matter how much
We try to arrange it?

135. When evil appears
The righteous must fight
With all of their strength
To defend what is right

136. Humanity's foe
Is unchecked desire
Together with anger -
Insatiable fire

137. Desire unchecked,
Says wisdom's consensus
Is identifying
With bodily senses

138. By discipline,
Control desire
Turn off that low self,
Reach for the Higher

139. Live Trudy live,
To fight and be wise
To love and to give
And to join the good guys

140. Trudy, you cannot
Transform everyone
But people can change,
And they do, one by one

141. You can't change the world
And everyone in it
You can change yourself.
That fight - you can win it.

142. Your mind is a force
You cannot elude
Learn to control it,
See it subdued

143. You know not yet
All you can give
Therefore, Trudy Newman,
Live!

144. You want to see
Mankind transformed
Evil vanquished,
By good informed

145. Be that virtue yourself,
Ms. Newman
Find within
Your shining human

146. Do the work
That is required
Let yourself
By God be hired

147. Within,
Dual possibilities dwell,
The world as heaven
Or as hell

148. Your mind forges chains
That make you feel bound
But you can use mind
To turn things around

149. Decide every day
To hark to the voice
Of silence within,
That gives you the choice

150. To decide how much leeway
To give to your mind
Try it and Trudy I tell you,
You'll find

151. A new way of living
That feels so much better
Than bound by those mind chains,
Bound by those fetters

152. True one, my dear one,
Take refuge in Me
Let Me run the world,
Feel safe and feel free

153. For now I will give you
A final epistle
Whenever you want Me,
Just inwardly whistle

154. I always am with you
Forever and ever
And ever and ever
And ever and ever

155. Trudy was new
Trudy was true

156. A true Trudy Newman
A woman, a human

157. Alive, alive O